Fermenting vol. 3: Milk Kefir

by Rashelle Johnson

D1041599

Disclaimer:

This information is provided for consumer informational and educational purposes only and may not reflect the most current information available. This book is sold with the understanding the author and/or publisher is not giving medical advice, nor should the information contained in this book replace medical advice, nor is it intended to diagnose or treat any disease, illness or other medical condition. Always consult your medical practitioner before making any dietary changes or treating or attempting to treat any medical condition.

This information does not cover all possible uses, precautions, interactions or adverse effects of the topics covered in this book. Do not disregard, avoid, or delay seeking medical advice because of something you may have read in this book. Always consult your doctor before adding herbs to your diet or applying them using any of the methods described herein.

While we endeavor to keep the information up to date and correct, we make no representations or warranties of any kind, express or implied, about the completeness, accuracy, reliability, suitability or availability with respect to the book or the information, products, services, or related graphics contained book for any purpose. Any reliance you place on such information is therefore strictly at your own risk.

It's important that you use good judgment when it comes to fermented food. Do not consume food you think may have gone bad bad because it looks, smells or tastes bad. The author claims no responsibility for any liability, loss or damage caused as a result of use of the information found in this book.

Dedication:

This book series is dedicated to all those who have discovered the many benefits of fermented food and beverages. I'd like to thank my friends and family, who were kind enough to taste test the recipes for this book. Thanks guys! I couldn't have done it without you.

Contents

Milk Kefir

Milk kefir is a powerful probiotic beverage made by inoculating milk with kefir cultures and letting the milk ferment at room temperature. The fermentation process usually takes 24 hours or less, provided conditions are right. Milk kefir has a lower pH than regular milk, which aids in the preservation of the milk because it creates an environment in which bad bacteria are less likely to grow.

Animal milk is the most common type of milk used to make milk kefir. Depending on where in the world you're at, kefir can be found that has been made from cow, goat, sheep and even camel milk. Milk alternatives like coconut milk and soy milk can also be used.

Traditional kefir is the consistency of thin yogurt and has a similar tangy flavor. Due to the carbon dioxide created during the fermentation process, kefir is effervescent. The longer it's left to ferment, the more carbonation it tends to have.

Like most drinks that are known throughout the world, milk kefir is known by a number of names, including the following:

- **Drink of the Prophet.**
- **Grains of the Prophet.**
- **Keefir.**
- **Kefer.**
- **Kefirs.**
- **Kefyras.**
- **Kephir.**

- **Kepi.**
- **Kewra.**
- **Kiaphur.**
- **Kippi.**
- **Knapon.**
- **Snow lotus.**
- **Talai.**
- **Tara.**
- **Tibetan mushrooms.**

The cultures used to ferment milk kefir are known as *kefir grains*. Kefir grains contain *lacto-bacteria*, which are bacteria that are beneficial to the human body, and yeasts— along with lipids, proteins and sugars—that act on the milk, partially digesting it and creating lactic acid from much of the lactose contained in the milk. It's the lactic acid that gives kefir its tangy flavor. Because much of the lactose in the milk is processed during fermentation, people who are lactose intolerant are often able to consume milk that's been fermented into kefir.

Milk kefir is classified as a *probiotic food*, meaning it contains living microorganisms able to survive in the digestive tract once consumed. The term *probiotic* means "life promoting," which is indicative of the health effects probiotic microorganisms have when consumed. They aid with digestion, bolster the immune system and create enzymes that help the body absorb large amounts of nutrients from all food entering the digestive tract, not just the kefir.

In addition to lactic acid, milk kefir is known to contain the following compounds:

- **Acetaldehyde.**
- **Acetic acid bacteria.**
- **Acetic acid.**
- **Carbon dioxide.**
- **Diacetyl.**
- **Ethanol.**
- **Polysaccharide.**
- **Folic acid.**
- **Free amino acids.**
- **Kefiran.**
- **Lacto-bacteria.**
- **Lipids.**
- **Milk proteins.**
- **Vitamins and minerals.**
- **Water.**
- **Yeasts.**

The exact level of each of these compounds found in an individual batch of kefir varies from batch to batch due to a number of environmental variables. The kefir grains the milk kefir is made from play a role in the final composition of kefir, as does the temperature at which the kefir is fermented, the length of time the kefir is allowed to ferment and the proximity to which fermenting kefir is placed in regards to other fermentations.

The History of Kefir

Kefir is thought to have originated in the northern region of the Caucasus Mountain range, which is a range of mountains that runs from the Black Sea to the Caspian Sea at the border of where Europe and Asia meet. Nomadic shepherds living and working in the Northern part of the range made and consumed kefir as a staple in their diet. They carried bags of kefir with them as they traveled the slopes and kept a watchful eye on their herds.

Legend has it the Islamic prophet Muhammad himself gave the first kefir grains to Orthodox Christians and showed them how to use them to create the first batches of kefir. The grains were revered amongst the tribes that held them and were kept a closely guarded secret. It was believed by some that revealing the secret of the grains handed down from the Prophet would destroy the ability of the grains to make kefir.

Traditionally, kefir was made by placing milk and kefir grains into a bag made of sheepskin and hanging it outside near an entrance to one's home. The bag was left to ferment in the sun during the daytime hours. It was brought inside in the evening and again hung near the door. As people passed the bag when they entered or left the room, they were required to give the bag a squeeze to mix the kefir grains and milk inside. The kefir grains were left inside the bag indefinitely and more milk would be added at the beginning or end of each day to replace the kefir that was consumed.

Kefir grains were treated as family heirlooms and were passed from family member to family member and from generation to generation. While strangers may have been allowed to taste kefir, rare was the stranger who was shown how it was made. It was believed that kefir grains held magical powers and to divulge their secret would somehow diminish that power.

Because the people of Caucasus Mountains were so tight-lipped about kefir, it was hardly known outside of the area for hundreds of years.

While kefir is known to have existed in the Caucasus Mountains for hundreds of years and may have existed for thousands of years, it didn't make its way out of the mountains until the beginning of the 20th century when a group of Russian physicians interested in the health benefits of kefir hired the Blandov brothers to obtain the grains. They, in turn, hired a beautiful young woman to court the prince of an area that produced kefir in order to get some of his seeds. In a made-for-the-movies plot twist, the prince kidnapped the woman and forced her hand in marriage.

The woman was rescued and the prince was brought before a court. His punishment was to hand over ten pounds of kefir grains, which he eventually did. By 1908, milk kefir was being produced and sold in Moscow, primarily to those who wanted to reap the health benefits associated with kefir in published scientific studies.

Kefir soon became the most popular drink in Russia. It eventually spread across the globe and is currently commercially manufactured world-wide. It hasn't quite caught on in the rest of the world like it did with the Eastern European states, but still stands as one of the most popular fermented milk drinks in the world.

What Are Kefir Grains?

Kefir "grains" aren't cereal grains, as people tend to assume when they first hear the name. They're actually symbiotic cultures that look nothing like the grains you're familiar with. Kefir grains are shaped like small cauliflower florets, running anywhere from 1 to 5 cm. in length. They're irregularly shaped and are soft and slimy to the touch. In warmer weather, kefir grains can stretch out and become long and stringy.

The color of a healthy grain of kefir ranges from white to pale yellow. Darker-colored grains are usually, but not always, grains that are in poor health. When kefir grains are used to culture liquids other than milk, they can take on the color of the liquid they're cultured in.

Kefir grains are tightly packed cultures of beneficial bacteria, yeasts, fats, proteins and sugar. No two kefir grains are alike. Each culture is made up of its own blend of bacteria, yeast and other compounds and is combined in a unique manner. The grains will take on bacteria from the environment around them, so grains used in one area of the world are vastly different from grains used in another. Each individual grain of kefir is in a constant state of flux, so you'll never find two grains made of exactly the same compounds.

For this reason, there's a lot of variance in how fast kefir grains produce kefir. Some grains are prolific fermenters, whipping out batch after batch of kefir and doing so in 12 hours or less. Other grains act slowly, taking 24 or even 48 hours to ferment the same amount of milk. This is natural and doesn't indicate a problem with the grains unless the change is sudden.

There are large numbers of beneficial bacteria and various yeasts found in kefir grains. Here are some of the probiotic organisms and yeasts found in kefir:

- *Acetobacter aceti.*
- *Acetobacter rasens.*
- *Candida famata.*
- *Candida kefyr.*
- *Candida lambica.*
- *Dekkera anomala.*
- *Galactomyces geotrichum.*
- *Kluyveromyces marxianus.*
- *Lactobacillus acidophilus.*
- *Lactobacillus brevis.*
- *Lactobacillus casei.*
- *Lactobacillus cellobiosus.*
- *Lactobacillus cremoris.*
- *Lactobacillus delbrueckii sub. bulgaricus.*
- *Lactobacillus fermentum.*
- *Lactobacillus frutivorans.*
- *Lactobacillus helveticus.*
- *Lactobacillus kefir.*
- *Lactobacillus kefirgranum.*
- *Lactobacillus kerifanofaciens.*
- *Lactobacillus paracasei.*
- *Lactobacillus parakefir.*
- *Lactobacillus plantarum.*

- *Lactococcus lactis sub. lactis biovar. diacetylactis.*
- *Lactococcus lactis sub. lactis.*
- *Lactococcus lactis sub. cremoris.*
- *Leuconostoc mesenteroides sub. cremoris.*
- *Leuconostoc mesenteroides sub. mesenteroides.*
- *Pichia fermentans.*
- *Saccharomyces cerevisiae.*
- *Saccharomyces unisporus.*
- *Streptococcus salivarius sub. thermophilus.*
- *Zygocaccharomyces.*

Keep in mind this is only a sampling of the bacteria found in milk kefir grains. There are over 50 strains known to exist in milk kefir grains and likely hundreds that haven't yet been discovered.

Each kefir grain is made up of a unique combination of bacteria and yeasts, along with lipids, proteins and a number of other organic compounds. The average kefir grain is made up of approximately 85% lacto-bacteria, 10% yeasts and 5% percent other compounds. The chemical composition of kefir grains, and as a result, kefir itself, is highly variable.

Kefir grains usually rest at the bottom of the fermenting container, but it isn't unheard of for some grains to float to the top. This usually isn't a problem, as the carbon dioxide produced by the yeast can get trapped inside the grains, making them buoyant. Damaged grains may also float. A lot of floating grains accompanied by poor quality kefir may be indicative of problems with the grains.

Healthy grains of kefir can last a lifetime.

They can be used to make batch after batch of kefir and will often begin producing "baby grains" the size of a grain of rice. As long as you supply your baby grains with a constant supply of fresh milk, they'll eventually propagate into larger grains. Make enough kefir and you'll eventually have more grains than you need. Give them away to friends or add them to smoothies for a powerful probiotic boost.

Powdered Starter Cultures

While searching out kefir grains, you may come across manufacturers selling powdered starter cultures that are artificially prepared. While these cultures will make a drink similar to kefir, they lack the biodiversity of true kefir grains. While kefir grains have a multitude of strains of bacteria and yeasts, the commercial powders usually only contain a handful of common probiotic bacteria strains and rarely have more than a single yeast strain.

Kefir grains are relatively inexpensive, so the only good reason to purchase powdered starter culture is if you only want to ferment the occasional batch of kefir and don't want to be bothered with storing and caring for kefir grains. Even then, you'd probably be better off buying already-prepared commercial kefir.

The biggest downside to powdered cultures for those looking to make multiple batches of kefir is the inability to continuously inoculate new batches of kefir with the same kefir grains. You may be able to inoculate a new batch of kefir with kefir left over from a batch made from powdered cultures, but this isn't sustainable long-term. You may get a handful of batches of kefir out of it, but you'll eventually need to use a new packet of cultures as the kefir gets weaker and weaker.

Another problem with powdered cultures is they can't be used to grow new kefir grains. Healthy kefir grains will often create new kefir grains during fermentation. Kefir grains don't form when powdered cultures are used to make milk kefir.

If you want a quick batch of fermented milk that tastes like kefir, powdered cultures can be a quick fix. If you want real milk kefir and all of its associated health benefits, go with kefir grains and you won't be sorry.

The Fermentation Process

When kefir grains are added to milk and the milk is left to ferment, the microflora in the grains go to work immediately. The various lactobacteria in the kefir grains start feeding on the lactose in the milk, converting the milk sugars to lactic acid. Yeasts in the kefir grains also start converting lactose, but they break it down into carbon dioxide and ethanol instead of lactic acid. Additionally, *acetic acid bacteria* may be present and may start creating acetic acid.

Lactic acid is the most abundant compound found in kefir after fermentation. It causes the milk to thicken by coagulating the casein (milk protein) in the milk. Lactic acid lowers the pH of the milk, making it acidic in nature. This is the reason fermented milk tastes sour and is the primary reason milk kefir has a longer shelf life than regular milk. Harmful pathogens have trouble growing in the lower pH environment.

Small amounts of *ethanol* are produced by the yeasts found in milk kefir grains. This is a natural byproduct of the fermentation process, and pretty much all fermented beverages have at least trace amounts of alcohol in them. The amount of alcohol in a batch of milk kefir varies, but is often less than 1% when traditional brewing methods are used. Some sources state milk kefir has less than 0.5% alcohol by volume, which would mean it's classified as a non-alcoholic beverage in the United States.

Kefir rarely reaches 2% alcohol by volume unless extended fermentation times are used and the lid on the fermenting container is tightly capped. Most kefir drinkers will tell you they've never so much as got a buzz from consuming kefir, as even strong kefir has less than half the alcohol by volume of a wine cooler.

The temperature range at which kefir can ferment is huge, ranging from 39 degrees F all the up to somewhere around 100 degrees F. While fermentation can take place at the extreme ends of the temperature range, problems are much more likely to occur. Low temperatures slow fermentation to a crawl, while high temperatures speed it up. The ideal temperature for fermenting is 74 degrees F, with anything in the 70 to 80 degree range being good. Get too much above 80 degrees F and you run the risk of doing permanent damage to your kefir grains.

If you live in a climate where ambient room temperatures are outside of the ideal range, kefir fermentation is still possible. You can ferment in a root cellar or a fridge during the heat of the day, moving the fermenting vessel out at night when the temperatures drop. Kefir can be left in the fridge to ferment, but it'll take 5 to 7 days instead of the usual 12 to 24 hours. You can also start fermentation with ice cold milk and place the container in an empty well-insulated ice chest, which should keep the temperature within the acceptable range for a 24-hour ferment.

Fermentation vessels need to be kept out of direct sunlight because they can heat the contents of the container to temperatures outside the acceptable range, even if the temperature inside the house is fine. Kefir does best in low-light environments, so keep your kefir somewhere it won't be exposed to direct light. This is especially important when fermenting in a clear glass container because sunlight can promote the growth of undesirable bacteria.

Fermentation time can vary depending on the effect you're trying to produce. Most ferments last somewhere between 12 and 48 hours. A shorter fermenting time will produce kefir that's thin and sweet, but has more lactose in it. Longer fermentation times will produce thick, tart kefir that is sour and has higher alcohol content.

Dual-fermentation is sometimes used to increase carbonation levels. During the first ferment, the kefir is allowed to ferment for 24 hours with the grains in it, after which time the grains are removed and the kefir is placed in a tightly-capped bottle. The kefir is then left to ferment for another 24- to 36-hour period, during which time carbon dioxide gas is created and trapped inside the bottle. This carbonates the kefir, giving it a satisfying fizz.

Be careful when using a tightly-capped bottle because a lot of pressure can build up. Use bottles with rubber gaskets to prevent the bottle from popping its lid or exploding and open the bottle at least once a day to release pressure. While fermenting milk kefir may not seem dangerous at a glance, there are reports of lids shooting violently off of bottles and anecdotes indicating glass bottles have shattered, sending glass flying everywhere.

Yogurt vs. Kefir

Since yogurt and kefir are both fermented milk products containing probiotic bacteria, people often assume they're pretty much the same thing. There are some similarities, but yogurt and kefir differ in a number of ways.

Yogurt and kefir are similar in taste and both have a consistent texture that's thicker than the milk they're made from, but kefir tends to be thinner. Kefir is usually consumed as a beverage, while yogurt is most often eaten with a spoon. Kefir is mildly carbonated, while yogurt isn't. While the alcohol content in milk kefir is usually low, yogurt doesn't contain the level of alcohol you find in kefir.

Kefir grains are used to culture milk kefir. Yogurt requires yogurt cultures, but there are no yogurt grains to move from batch to batch. Instead, a few tablespoons of the previous batch are added to the new batch or a starter culture is used. There are dried and powdered cultures available for both yogurt and kefir, but in the case of kefir they aren't as effective as the grains.

There are different bacteria found in yogurt than there are in kefir. There are fewer bacteria strains found in yogurt, and the most common types aren't likely to stick around for long in the digestive tract. Kefir contains many more varieties of bacteria, some of which may take up residence in the intestines. Kefir is clearly the more biodiverse choice when it comes to beneficial bacteria. It contains many of the same bacteria found in yogurt, plus adds quite a few of its own to the mix.

Kefir also contains a number of yeasts not found in yogurt. These yeasts, along with the bacteria, release enzymes that aid with digestion and help the body process lactose. The yeasts found in kefir seek and destroy pathogenic yeasts in the body, and in doing so make the immune system stronger.

Another key difference between yogurt and kefir lies in the fermentation process. Some yogurt varieties can be cultured at room temperature, while others have to be heated to properly form. Milk kefir is always fermented at room temperature.

Store-bought yogurt contains added sugar and artificial additives that kill a lot of the health value of the yogurt. Check the labels closely because you're getting a lot more than you bargained for. If you're making your yogurt at home, it's better for you than the store-bought stuff, but still isn't as healthy as kefir. When buying yogurt or kefir from the store, make sure you're getting the probiotic version that contains live cultures.

The good news is you don't have to choose one over the other. The beneficial bacteria found in yogurt work together with the bacteria in milk kefir to keep your gut working like a fine-tuned machine. Consuming both is beneficial, as long as you don't eat too much of the store-bought sugar-filled yogurt.

The Health Benefits of Milk Kefir

Kefir is a powerful probiotic food that some say should be deemed a superfood. Although kefir has been around for hundreds—and possibly thousands—of years, research into the many health benefits of milk kefir is still in its infancy.

Here are some of the health benefits milk kefir is said to have:

- **Aids with digestion.**
- **Allergy relief.**
- **Asthma relief.**
- **Bone health.**
- **Cleanses the digestive tract.**
- **Cold and flu relief.**
- **Contains high levels of biotin, thiamin, vitamin B12, calcium and vitamin K2.**
- **Diarrhea relief.**
- **Eliminates constipation.**
- **Helps balance bacterial flora in the body.**
- **Helps knock down yeast infections.**
- **Helps the lactose intolerant digest dairy.**
- **Helps with gastrointestinal issues.**
- **High in protein.**
- **Immune system boost.**
- **Reduces acne.**
- **Replace bacteria in the digestive tract that are killed off when antibiotics are taken.**
- **Sleep aid.**
- **Those who drink it generally feel better.**

- **Ulcer relief.**

In addition to the above health benefits, milk kefir also helps those who drink it obtain as much nourishment as possible from the food they eat. The bacteria, yeasts and enzymes help the body break down and absorb larger amounts of nutrients from food.

What Kind of Milk Should You Use?

The best kefir I've ever tasted was made from raw organic milk fresh off a farm where the cows are allowed to roam free and eat grass. Raw milk is unprocessed milk that's basically delivered straight from the cow to you. It's supposed to be better for you and there are a large group of people who believe it's the only way to drink milk.

Any discussion of raw milk wouldn't be complete without discussion of the safety aspect. There's a good reason why raw milk is banned in a number of jurisdiction, and that's the worry of contamination. Raw milk has to be procured in a safe and hygienic manner or there's a real risk of harmful pathogens developing. Unless you're sure the raw milk you're getting is from a reputable source, stick to pasteurized milk.

Unless you own a goat, sheep or dairy cow, raw milk may be difficult to find. It's heavily regulated and is outright banned in some areas of the world. Luckily for those who aren't able to get raw milk, there are other options that make kefir that's almost as good.

The milk that's sold in most stores is pasteurized milk, meaning it's been heated to 160 degrees F and held there for a short time in order to kill any pathogens or bacteria in the milk. This increases the shelf life at the cost of all the beneficial bacteria and some vitamins and minerals. Pasteurized milk is a virtual dead zone when it comes to microorganisms, but that doesn't mean they can't be added back in. Pasteurized milk can be used to make kefir and the kefir made from it is pretty good.

If you have a dairy nearby, you might be able to purchase pasteurized milk directly from the dairy. Fresh pasteurized milk is the best milk to use.

Ultra-pasteurized milk is milk that's heated even more than pasteurized milk. It's typically heated to 275 degrees F and is held there for a couple seconds. This process allows for an extended shelf life, but changes the taste of the milk and reduces the vitamin and mineral content. There are quite a few sources that state kefir can't be made from this type of milk. It can, but I've found it tastes a little off when compared to kefir made with other milk types. Your mileage may vary.

Both homogenized and non-homogenized milk can be used to make kefir. Homogenized milk has been treated to break the fat in the milk into tiny pieces to prevent the cream from separating and rising to the top. When you make kefir from non-homogenized milk, there will be a layer of fermented cream at the top of the container.

Kefir can be made from the milk of pretty much any animal you can draw milk from. Cow, goat and sheep milk are the most common milk types for kefir, but it's also made from camel, buffalo and llama milk. There are even parents who make human breast milk kefir for their lactose-intolerant babies. If you're able to milk an animal, you can probably make kefir with the milk.

The fat content of the milk doesn't matter as far as fermenting goes. Fat-free milk will ferment every bit as well as whole milk, with the difference being whole milk kefir will be thicker than fat-free milk kefir.

There are a number of non-dairy milk substitutes that can be used to make milk kefir using the same milk kefir grains used to ferment animal milk. The results may not be as consistent as with animal milk, but the following milk substitutes can be used to make kefir:

- **Almond milk.**
- **Coconut milk.**
- **Hemp milk.**
- **Nut milks.**
- **Oat milk.**
- **Rice milk.**
- **Seed milks.**
- **Soy milk.**

While kefir grains can be used in all sorts of alternative milks, they need animal milk to grow and thrive. Return the kefir grains to animal milk every couple weeks and let them sit for a day in order to bring them back to life. You'll know your grains are getting tired when the kefir they make starts to weaken and takes longer than normal to ferment. When this occurs, it's time to move them back to animal milk for a day or two.

Kefir Culturing Vessels

When it comes to the container used to culture kefir, you can keep it simple or you can get as elaborate as you'd like. There are several concerns you need to keep in mind when deciding what type of container you're going to use.

Kefir is acidic by nature and will react to some materials, so it's important a non-reactive container material is used. This rules out many plastic and most metal containers right from the get-go. Reactive containers will leach chemicals into the kefir during the fermentation process because the acids in the kefir start chemically reacting to the chemical compounds the container is made of.

Non-reactive container materials include glass, some plastics, ceramic and porcelain. Ceramic doesn't react to kefir, but it's important to be sure the glaze used on the ceramic doesn't contain lead because it can leach out. Plastic can also contain chemicals you don't want in your kefir. Stainless steel is mentioned by some literature as being non-reactive. It's as non-reactive as metal gets and some people do successfully use it to make kefir, but it will eventually start to react to the acids in kefir.

Of all the container materials you can choose from, glass is by far the best choice. It's as non-reactive a material as you can get. The containers aren't easily damaged (unless you drop one) and they aren't loaded with chemicals or lead that can leach into the final product. They're also inexpensive and easy to clean.

While there are a number of specialty containers on the market that can be used to good effect, all you really need to make kefir are a few quart or half-gallon canning jars and some bottles with lids with rubber gaskets. There's no need to break the bank on kefir culturing supplies. Remember, kefir was originally made in bags made from animal skin. Any container you use is a step up from that.

Traditional Kefir

There are two basic kefir recipes you need to know how to make in order to make the rest of the recipes in the book. The first recipe is traditional kefir. Every single recipe in this book is a variation of this kefir recipe. The liquids used may be different and the fermenting times may change, but the basic steps and technique is the same. Once you've got this recipe (and the next one) down, the rest of the recipes in the book will be a breeze because they all build on one of these two recipes.

Here are the supplies you're going to need to make traditional kefir:

- **Milk kefir grains.**
- **A fermenting vessel.**
- **Milk.**
- **A stainless steel fine mesh strainer.**

That's it. Those are the only 4 items you're going to need to make your first batch of milk kefir. Easy, right?

Kefir grains can be obtained from a number of sources. The best grains come from friends and family members who have kefir cultures growing at home. If you know someone who brews kefir, ask them if they've got any extra grains they're willing to pass on to you. If you don't know anyone who makes kefir, you're going to have to source them online or from a local health food store. I've found health food stores can be hit and miss when it comes to supply and quality, so your best bet is to find a good supplier online.

See the previous chapter for help choosing a fermenting vessel. Glass is your best bet. If you're using kefir grains purchased online or from a store, they're probably going to be a bit weak at first. Start by fermenting small amounts of kefir in a pint-sized container until the grains wake up.

Start with a tablespoon or two of grains. Place the grains in a pint of organic cow's milk and leave them to ferment for 24 hours. If the kefir is good, it can be consumed and you can try making larger amounts of kefir with your grains. If the kefir isn't good after 24 hours, swap out the milk and wait another 24 hours. Continue switching out the milk every 24 hours until the kefir grains have revived and are making good pints of kefir.

The grains can take up to 14 days to revive. If they haven't come back to life after a week, they may be damaged beyond repair. Contact the supplier and ask for a new set of grains.

If you'd like more kefir, 2 tablespoons of active grains are all it usually takes to ferment a quart of milk. If you don't have 2 tablespoons of grains, continue making kefir by the pint until you do have enough grains. In some cases, it may only take a tablespoon of highly active grains to ferment a quart of kefir. It depends on how strong the grains are and figuring out how many grains you need is going to require some fine-tuning.

Here are the instructions for making traditional kefir once you have active kefir grains. These instructions assume you're making a quart of kefir and are using a glass quart-sized canning jar:

1. Pour 4 cups of milk into a quart-sized glass canning jar.
2. Add 2 tablespoons of kefir grains to the jar and stir the contents with a wood or plastic spoon. Make sure you use a non-reactive spoon or cup to move the kefir grains to the jar.
3. Cover the container with some sort of breathable fiber. Cotton cloth, cheesecloth or even a large coffee filter can be used to cover the container. The idea is to let air in while keeping insects out. Tie the cloth to the container or use a rubber band to attach it so it won't come off.
4. Let the container sit at room temperature for 24 hours.
5. Check the kefir every 12 hours to see if it's done. If it isn't done after 24 hours, it can be allowed to ferment for an additional 24 hours. Check it every 6 to 12 hours after the first 24-hours have passed. You can stir the kefir each time you check it if you'd like, but it usually isn't necessary.
6. Once the kefir is done, strain out the grains using a clean stainless steel fine mesh strainer. Don't leave the grains in the kefir past the 48-hour mark or you run the risk of damaging the grains. Move the grains to a new container full of milk to ensure they stay fed.
7. Once the kefir is done fermenting, place a tight lid on the container (or bottle the kefir in glass bottles with lids with rubber gaskets) and move the kefir to the fridge. This will slow

fermentation to a crawl and will further preserve the kefir.

This simple kefir is the basis for the rest of the recipes in this book. You can consume it as-is or you can add to it or change the type of milk as you see fit. It varies from batch to batch, but this kefir is usually lightly sour with a hint of sweetness. It's only slightly carbonated, so if you want more carbonation, you're going to have to make the next recipe.

Vanilla Milk Kefir

I'm a little embarrassed to admit I didn't think of this one myself. It's such a simple addition and it really improves the taste of the kefir. My husband wondered aloud one day whether kefir would taste good with vanilla extract added to it. We tried it, and it did. On days when I'm craving something sweet, I make this recipe and drizzle caramel over the top. It's sinfully delicious.

There are only 2 ingredients required for this recipe:

- **2 cups milk kefir.**
- **1 to 2 teaspoons vanilla extract.**

Stir the vanilla extract into the milk kefir. Enjoy.

Sweet Maple Kefir

Add maple syrup to traditional kefir to get sweet kefir that can be used in place of traditional kefir in recipes you want to add a bit of sweetness to. I've seen honey used to sweeten kefir, but prefer not to use it unless I'm planning on using the kefir immediately. Honey has mild antibacterial properties and may kill off the beneficial bacteria in kefir if left to sit for too long.

Here are the ingredients you'll need:

- **2 cups traditional milk kefir.**
- **Organic maple syrup, to taste.**

This one's easy. Stir the maple syrup into the milk kefir. Taste it and add more syrup if it isn't sweet enough.

Citrus Kefir

While most people wouldn't consider squeezing a lemon, an orange or a lime into a glass of milk and drinking it, citrus goes surprisingly well with milk kefir. This recipe is in the traditional kefir section, but is every bit as good when it's fermented a second time to make it into a fizzy kefir.

You need two items to make citrus kefir:

- **2 cups milk kefir.**
- **2 to 4 tablespoons citrus juice.**

Blend the citrus juice into the milk kefir and serve immediately.

Cocoa Spice Milk Kefir

Cocoa is another simple addition to kefir that makes it taste great. You can add just cocoa to get a great tasting chocolate kefir. This recipe takes it a step further, creating a spicy cocoa kefir that tastes divine.

You're going to need these supplies:

- **4 cups milk kefir.**
- **5 tablespoons cocoa powder.**
- **2 cloves.**
- **2 tablespoons ground cinnamon.**
- **¼ tablespoon nutmeg.**
- **Organic cane sugar or stevia, to taste.**

Here are the instructions for creating cocoa spice milk kefir:

1. Make traditional milk kefir, letting the kefir ferment at room temperature for 24 hours.
2. Strain out the kefir grains and move them to fresh milk.
3. Add the cocoa powder, cloves, cinnamon and nutmeg and stir them into the kefir.
4. Place a lid on the kefir and let it ferment for an addition 12 to 24 hours.
5. Add sweetener, to taste, and place an airtight lid on the container and move it to the fridge.

Rise and Shine Kefir

This kefir uses both carrots and carrot juice to create a kefir that's great in the morning. It's also great for an afternoon snack, or any other time you want kefir, for that matter. The shredded carrot is filling, which makes this kefir a great choice as a meal replacement for those looking to lose weight. Just go easy on the sweetener, as you don't want to add too many calories.

Here are the supplies you're going to need:

- **2 cups milk kefir.**
- **½ cup carrot juice.**
- **½ cup shredded carrots.**
- **1 teaspoon vanilla extract.**
- **Sweetener, to taste.**
- **Fermenting vessel.**

Here are the instructions for making rise and shine kefir:

1. Make traditional milk kefir. The first ferment should last 12 to 24 hours. Strain out the kefir grains before adding any of the other ingredients to the fermenting vessel.
2. Place the milk kefir in the fermenting vessel and add the carrots, carrot juice and vanilla extract to the container.
3. Place a lid on the container and allow it to ferment for an additional 12 to 24 hours.
4. Move the container to the fridge until you're ready to consume the kefir.
5. Right before serving, place the kefir in the blender and blend everything together. Add

sweetener, to taste. Stevia and rapadura are both good choices for sweetener.

Kefir Protein Power Shake

Bodybuilders and those looking to stay or get fit are constantly on the hunt for good ways to add protein to their diet. This recipe combines the protein in milk kefir with a scoop or two of protein powder to give those who drink it a super-boost of protein. This shake works best when consumed right before or right after working out.

This recipe works well with most flavors of protein powder. I've tried it with cookies and cream, vanilla and chocolate protein powder and all three have been good.

Here are the ingredients:

- **1 ½ cups milk kefir.**
- **1 – 2 scoops of your favorite protein powder blend.**
- **½ cup milk.**

Place all of the ingredients in a large shaker bottle and shake until blended. Drink immediately.

Kefir Raspberry Flaxseed Fiber Booster

Fiber is key to ensuring your digestive system functions properly. Adding fiber to the probiotic bacteria in kefir gives your digestive system an extra boost and gets things moving along nicely, if you know what I mean. Raspberries are naturally high in fiber. So is flaxseed. Combining them both with kefir adds insoluble dietary fiber to your diet in an easy to drink and tasty package.

Here are the ingredients you're going to need to make the fiber booster:

- **2 cups milk kefir.**
- **2 tablespoons ground flaxseed.**
- **½ cup raspberries.**
- **Organic cane sugar, to taste (optional).**

Combine the ingredients in a blender and blend them together. Add sweetener if you'd like. Serve immediately.

Sweet Lavender Milk Kefir

Lavender wasn't something I expected would go well with milk kefir. One day I had extra lavender flower heads laying around and I looked at my fermenting kefir and thought, *what the heck, might as well*. I'm glad I did because this is the kefir I reach for after a stressful day. It helps me relax and destress.

Lavender essential oil can be added to the kefir instead of the flower heads. Be careful when using essential oils because they are very powerful. Use therapeutic grade oil and only use a couple drops.

There are only a handful of ingredients needed to make this recipe:

- **4 cups milk kefir.**
- **2 tablespoons dried lavender flower heads.**
- **Organic cane sugar or stevia, to taste.**

Follow these steps to make sweet lavender milk kefir:

1. Make traditional milk kefir, letting the kefir ferment at room temperature for 24 hours.
2. Strain out the kefir grains and move them to fresh milk.
3. Stir the lavender flower heads into the milk kefir. Do not add the flower heads while the kefir grains are still in the kefir.
4. Place the lid on the kefir and let it sit at room temperature overnight. The second ferment should last 12 to 24 hours.
5. Strain the kefir to get rid of the flower heads.

6. Add cane sugar or stevia, to taste. Stir the sweetener into the kefir.
7. Place the kefir in an airtight container in the fridge.

Sweet Raspberry Milk Kefir

This recipe calls for raspberry preserves. It could just have easily used any other flavor of preserve, jelly or jam. The more you use, the sweeter the kefir will be.

Here are the supplies you'll need on hand:

- **2 cups milk kefir.**
- **3 tablespoons raspberry preserves (or more, if you'd like).**
- **Blender.**

Here's how to make it:

1. Place the milk kefir and the raspberry preserves in the blender.
2. Blend them together.
3. Serve immediately. You can blend ice into the kefir if you want it to be like a smoothie, or you can pour it over ice cubes.

Strawberry Banana Kefir Smoothie

There are 2 ways to make a kefir smoothie. The first is to use milk kefir as the liquid in the smoothie. You can use milk kefir to replace water or milk in most smoothie recipes.

The second method is to take any excess kefir grains you have on hand and blend them directly into the smoothie. Kefir grains are edible and are packed with probiotic cultures. You won't be able to do this every time you make a smoothie, but it does make for an occasional special treat if you make a lot of kefir and have extra grains on hand.

Here are the ingredients needed to make a strawberry banana kefir smoothie:

- **1 cup milk kefir.**
- **6 to 8 strawberries.**
- **1 banana.**
- **5 ice cubes.**

Add all of the ingredients to a blender and blend them together. Serve immediately.

Strawberry Lime Kefir Smoothie

This delicious smoothie tastes like strawberries and has a tangy citrus bite to it. You can use lime juice, or you can peel a lime and toss the entire lime into the blender. It's a bit sour as-is, so don't be afraid to add a bit of organic cane sugar to the recipe to sweeten it up a bit.

Here are the ingredients:

- **1 cup milk kefir.**
- **2 tablespoons lime juice (or a whole lime).**
- **5 strawberries.**
- **Organic cane sugar, to taste (optional).**
- **5 ice cubes.**

Add everything to a blender and blend it all together. Add sugar, to taste.

Watermelon Slush Kefir Smoothie

Here's one for a hot summer day. This smoothie is delicious and is relatively low in calories, making it a great choice for those looking to lose weight.

Here are the ingredients:

- **1 cup milk kefir.**
- **2 cups seedless watermelon, chopped.**
- **10 ice cubes.**

Add everything to a blender and blend it all together. Serve immediately.

Piña Colada Kefir

Piña colada kefir can be served without alcohol, or you can add 2 to 3 ounces of white rum to it to make it a real cocktail. This recipe has been a big hit at my house during parties. The only problem is you can't make more when you run out of kefir.

Here are the supplies you'll need on hand:

- **1 cups milk kefir.**
- **½ cup coconut cream.**
- **½ cup pineapple juice.**
- **Blender.**

Here's how to make it:

1. Place the milk kefir, coconut cream and pineapple juice in the blender.
2. Blend them together.
3. Serve immediately. You can blend ice into the kefir if you want it to be like a smoothie, or you can pour it over ice cubes.

Pumpkin Pie Kefir

Pumpkin pie kefir is a tasty treat I like to serve around the holidays. My family loves this recipe and the kids beg for it year-round. This recipe explains how to make pumpkin pie kefir using real pumpkin. It's one of the more difficult recipes in this book when you use real pumpkin. You can speed things up by using canned pumpkin.

Here are the supplies you'll need:

- **1 small pumpkin.**
- **A knife.**
- **A blender.**
- **A cookie sheet.**
- **4 cups milk kefir.**
- **1 teaspoon vanilla extract.**
- **½ teaspoon cinnamon.**
- **½ teaspoon nutmeg.**

Follow these instructions to make this recipe:

1. Cut the stem off of the pumpkin.
2. Slice the pumpkin in half and scoop out the innards. Remove as much of the seeds and pulp as humanly possible. A few strings left behind aren't going to kill anyone.
3. Chop the pumpkin into chunks.
4. Place the pumpkin on a cookie sheet and roast the pumpkin at 350 degrees F until the pieces are soft. This usually takes between 45 minutes and an hour.
5. Let the pumpkin cool.

6. Remove the skin from the pumpkin and discard the skin.
7. Place the pumpkin flesh into the blender and blend until smooth. A good blender will puree the pumpkin without having to add water. You can add a bit of water if you need to.
8. Blend the pumpkin until it's completely smooth.
9. Add 1 cup of the blended pumpkin to 4 cups of milk kefir.
10. Stir in the vanilla, cinnamon and nutmeg.
11. Sprinkle cinnamon on top and serve cold.

Kefir Egg Nog

What good would pumpkin pie be without egg nog to accompany it? Kefir egg nog, that is. This recipe is close enough to the real thing that I've served it to my family without them realizing it was made with kefir.

Here are the ingredients you're going to need to make kefir egg nog:

- **4 cups traditional kefir.**
- **2 eggs.**
- **2 to 3 tablespoons organic cane sugar.**
- **½ teaspoon cinnamon.**
- **½ teaspoon nutmeg.**

Here are the directions for this recipe:

1. Combine the kefir, eggs, sugar, cinnamon and nutmeg in a blender and pulse until completely smooth.
2. Sprinkle a bit of nutmeg mixed with cinnamon on top of each cup as you pour it.
3. Serve immediately.

Chai-Infused Kefir

The word *chai* directly translates to "tea" in many parts of the world. It's an age-old beverage that has its roots in India. Chai, as we know it in the States, is generally made up of black tea mixed with various Indian spices. Cardamom, ginger and cinnamon are all common spices used in chai tea.

For this recipe, you can use either a chai teabag or you can place the chai directly in the kefir. If you're using a teabag, make sure it isn't stapled shut. The metal staple could react with the kefir and product unpredictable results.

Gather these supplies prior to making chai-infused kefir:

- **2 cups milk kefir.**
- **Chai tea (either 1 teabag or 2 tablespoons of loose tea).**
- **Maple syrup, to taste.**
- **Fermenting vessel.**

Follow these directions to infuse your kefir with the flavor of chai:

1. Use only freshly-fermented kefir for this recipe. Strain out the kefir grains prior to adding the chai tea. Place the kefir in a fermenting vessel.
2. Add the chai tea to the kefir. If the tea is loose, mix it into the kefir. If it's a teabag, place the teabag into the kefir.
3. Place a tight lid on the container and let it sit at room temperature for up to 24 hours.

4. Once the tea has fermented to your liking, either remove the tea bag or strain the tea out of the kefir. Move the kefir to the fridge and store it in an airtight container until you're ready to drink it.

5. When you're ready to drink the tea, add sweetener to it, to taste.

Kefir Chocolate Pudding

Are you looking for a probiotic chocolate pudding recipe? Probably not, but once you've tried this one, you aren't going to want to eat regular pudding again. Try adding flax seeds or chia seeds to this recipe to make it even better for you.

Here are the supplies you'll need to make kefir chocolate pudding:

- **2 cups milk kefir.**
- **¼ cup maple syrup, or a few drops of stevia, to taste.**
- **2 avocados.**
- **4 tablespoons cocoa powder.**

The directions for this one are simple. Place all the ingredients in a blender and blend them together until the consistency of pudding. This recipe doesn't store well and should be served immediately.

Kefir Peanut Butter Banana Pudding

Here's another great tasting pudding recipe you didn't know you needed until now. This recipe is delicious on its own, or you can add a couple tablespoons of cocoa powder to make chocolate peanut butter banana pudding.

Here are the supplies you need:

- **2 cups milk kefir.**
- **¼ cup maple syrup, or a few drops of stevia, to taste.**
- **2 avocados.**
- **3 tablespoons peanut butter.**
- **1 ripe banana.**

The directions are the same as for the kefir chocolate pudding. Add everything to a blender and blend it all together. Freeze the banana first for chilled pudding. Again, this recipe doesn't store well and should be served immediately.

Kefir Cottage Cheese

This recipe uses whole milk and kefir to create cheese curds similar in taste and texture to cottage cheese. Be aware that heating the kefir as is done in this recipe will kill off most of the probiotic cultures.

Here are the supplies you need to make kefir cottage cheese:

- **8 cups fresh whole milk.**
- **2 cups kefir.**
- **1 teaspoon sea salt.**
- **Metal strainer.**

Follow these directions to make kefir cottage cheese:

1. When you ferment the kefir for this recipe, let the kefir ferment for 36 to 48 hours. You want the kefir to be very sour.
2. Place the milk in a pot and heat it to between 130 and 140 degrees F.
3. Pour the kefir in at a slow rate of speed while stirring the contents of the pot slowly. Curds will start to form. Be careful not to stir too hard and break up the curds. If curds aren't forming, turn the heat up a little bit at a time until they do.
4. Keep stirring until the curds have separated from the whey.
5. Strain the curds from the whey.
6. Place the curds in cheesecloth and let the whey drain out into a bowl.
7. Fold the sea salt into the kefir cottage cheese curds.

The whey that's left over won't contain much by way of beneficial flora because of the heat used to cause the milk to curdle. If you want to use the way as a starter culture to ferment vegetables or other foods, you can use a tablespoon or two of milk kefir grains to culture the way by fermenting it overnight the same way you would milk kefir.

Kefir Banana Peach Breakfast

Sometimes you're in a hurry in the morning and don't have time to make breakfast. Instead of reaching for a box of sugar cereal, make this tasty and healthy breakfast kefir dish.

Here are the ingredients:

- **½ cup milk kefir.**
- **1 cup kefir cottage cheese.**
- **1 banana.**
- **1 peach.**
- **2 tablespoons of honey.**

Here are the directions:

1. Combine the milk kefir and the cottage cheese and stir them together until blended.
2. Cut up the banana and the peach and stir them into the kefir.
3. Drizzle honey on top.
4. Enjoy.

Kefir and Granola

Here's another quick and easy breakfast for those days you're on the run. There are only two ingredients in this recipe, but you can improvise and add all sorts of fruit to make it even healthier. If you want to mask the sourness of the milk kefir, drizzle a couple teaspoons of honey on top of the kefir.

Here are just some of the types of fruit you can add:

- **Sliced peaches.**
- **Sliced nectarines.**
- **Sliced strawberries.**
- **Fresh bananas.**
- **Dried bananas.**
- **Raisins.**
- **Blueberries.**
- **Blackberries.**
- **Raspberries.**
- **Dried cranberries.**

Here are the two ingredients you'll need:

- **1 cup milk kefir.**
- **1 cup of your favorite granola.**

Here are the directions:

1. Place the milk kefir in the cup or bowl first.
2. If you're adding fruit, mix it into the kefir.
3. Pour the granola on top and serve immediately.

Fizzy Kefir

Sometimes you want kefir with a bit more carbonation. Fizzy kefir is made the same way as traditional kefir with one additional step. The carbonation is added via dual-fermentation, which means a second fermenting period is added after the first. This ferment is done without the milk kefir grains.

A tight lid is placed on the container to allow carbon dioxide gas to build up in the container. This carbon dioxide gas is what gives kefir its effervescent mouthfeel. The longer the second ferment lasts, the more carbonation there will be in the kefir. Be aware that extreme pressure can build up in the bottle. The lid can blow off the bottle and bottles might explode, sending glass everywhere if allowed to ferment for too long. Using containers with lids with rubber gaskets that expand under pressure can help alleviate this danger. It also helps to open the container at least once a day to release pressure.

The supplies you need for making for making fizzy kefir are the same as what you need for traditional kefir:

- **Milk kefir grains.**
- **A fermenting vessel.**
- **Milk.**
- **A stainless steel fine mesh strainer.**

The only difference is you need to make sure you have a container or bottles you can seal tightly for the second fermenting period.

Here are the instructions for making fizzy kefir:

1. Pour 4 cups of milk into a quart-sized glass canning jar.
2. Add 2 tablespoons of kefir grains to the jar and stir the contents with a wood or plastic spoon. Make sure you use a non-reactive spoon or cup to move the kefir grains to the jar.
3. Cover the container with some sort of breathable fiber. Cotton cloth, cheesecloth or even a large coffee filter can be used to cover the container. The idea is to let air in while keeping insects out. Tie the cloth to the container or use a rubber band to attach it so it won't come off.
4. Let the container sit at room temperature for 24 hours.
5. Check the kefir every 12 hours to see if it's done. If it isn't done after 24 hours, it can be allowed to ferment for an additional 24 to 36 hours. Check it every 6 to 12 hours after the first 24-hours have passed. You can stir the kefir each time you check it if you'd like, but it usually isn't necessary.
6. Once the kefir is done with the first ferment, strain out the grains using a clean stainless steel fine mesh strainer. Don't leave the grains in the kefir past the 48-hour mark or you run the risk of damaging the grains. Move the grains to a new container full of milk to ensure they stay fed.
7. Once the kefir is done with the first ferment and the grains have been strained out, place a tight

lid on the container. Alternatively, the kefir can be placed in bottles that can be tightly capped.

8. Let the kefir ferment again, this time for an addition 12 to 24 hours. Remove the lid at least once a day to let any gases that build up escape. It's a good idea to release the lid while holding the container in the sink. The gases that build up can sometimes cause kefir to spray everywhere. If you've ever shaken a soda up and opened it, you know what I mean.

9. Once the kefir has fermented to your liking, it can be moved to the fridge. This will slow the fermentation process to a crawl and will prolong the life of the kefir.

Kefir made using a dual-fermentation process will have marginally more alcohol in it than single-fermented kefir. The longer the kefir is fermented, the more alcohol it will have. It'll also have more fizz, to a point.

Kefir Creamy Fruit Juice Soda

Combine fizzy kefir with fruit juice and what do you get? A concoction I call the kefir creamy fruit juice soda. Yes, it's a mouthful to say, but rest assured this one's a winner. It's one of the few kefir recipes kids enjoy.

Don't add the juice to the kefir while it's fermenting with the grains in it. Fruit juice often contains antibacterial compounds that can damage or destroy kefir grains. Juice should not be added to kefir (or vice versa, as is the case in this recipe) until after the grains have been strained out.

Here are the supplies needed to make this recipe:

- **1 cup juice.**
- **2 cups fizzy kefir.**
- **Large glass cup, for serving.**
- **Ice cubes.**
- **A dollop of whipped cream (optional).**

Here are the steps require to make this tasty cultured beverage:

1. Fill the cup with ice.
2. Pour 1 cup of fruit juice over the ice. Grape, cranberry, mango, orange, lemon and lime juice all work well. Don't be afraid to experiment with your favorite juices.
3. Pour the kefir into the cup over the top of the fruit juice.
4. Add a dollop of whipped cream to the top and serve immediately.

Kefir Italian Soda

If I had to choose a favorite milk kefir recipe, this would be it. I didn't know what an Italian Soda was until a few years back when I had one at a friend's house. Fast-forward three years and they're my go-to dessert when I'm craving something fizzy and sweet.

You can add sweetener to this recipe if you want it sweeter, but I've never had to. I like it just the way it is.

First, gather these supplies:

- **1 cup fizzy kefir.**
- **1 to 2 tablespoons flavored syrup.**
- **Half and half, to taste.**
- **Ice cubes.**

Next, follow these directions:

1. Fill a cup to the top with ice cubes.
2. Pour the flavored syrup over the ice. Fruit flavored syrups work well for Italian Soda. Chocolate syrup is delicious.
3. Fill the cup to within a couple inches of the top with fizzy kefir.
4. Add as much half and half as you'd like to the top.
5. Serve immediately.

Cinnamon Milk Kefir

Traditionally, both cinnamon and nuts have been sprinkled on top of milk kefir when it's served. This recipe adds the cinnamon to the milk kefir instead of simply sprinkling it on top.

Here's what you're going to need to whip up a batch of cinnamon milk kefir:

- **4 cups milk.**
- **1 to 2 tablespoons milk kefir grains.**
- **1 cinnamon stick.**
- **Fermenting vessel.**
- **½ teaspoon ground cinnamon.**

Here are the steps for making cinnamon milk kefir:

1. Place the milk kefir grains and the milk into the fermenting vessel. Cover the container with cloth and attach the cloth to the container. Ferment at room temperature for 12 to 24 hours.
2. Strain out the milk kefir grains and transfer them to a new container of milk.
3. Add the cinnamon stick to the fermenting vessel.
4. Place a tight lid on the container and let ferment for another 12 to 24 hours.
5. Take the lid off of the container and stir the contents of the container. Replace the lid.
6. Leave the cinnamon stick in the kefir and place the container in the fridge.
7. Sprinkle with ground cinnamon before serving.

Cocoa Cherry Fizzy Kefir

Cocoa cherry fizzy kefir is a family favorite and is one of the few kefir drinks my entire family agrees is delicious. Ferment the kefir for at least 24 hours the first ferment and an additional 24 hours the second ferment to ensure it has plenty of fizz.

Gather these ingredients before getting started:

- **4 cups milk kefir.**
- **¼ cup cocoa powder.**
- **1 cup organic cherries, pitted and halved.**
- **Fermenting vessel.**

Follow these instructions to make this recipe:

1. Always use fresh milk kefir that has just gone through the first fermenting period for this recipe. In order for dual-fermentation to work, the fermenting periods need to be back-to-back. Make sure the kefir grains have been strained out before you add the cherries and cocoa powder.
2. Once the kefir grains have been strained out, add the milk kefir, cocoa powder and cherries to the fermenting vessel and stir them all together. The cocoa should be stirred into the kefir.
3. Place a tight-fitting lid on the container and let the container sit at room temperature for an additional 12 to 24 hours for the second ferment.
4. Place the contents of the fermenting vessel in a blender and blend it up.
5. Tightly cap the container or bottle the kefir and store it in the fridge. Serve over ice.

Strawberry Milkshake Kefir

This recipe tastes like a slightly sour strawberry milkshake, with a touch of carbonation as an added bonus. If you've ever had an Italian Cream Soda, this recipe tastes similar. For those who haven't had one, cream is poured over carbonated water mixed with flavored syrup. They're good, but not really good for you. This recipe is a great compromise.

This recipe calls for ice cream, which isn't exactly good for you. You can use kefir cultured ice cream. There's a recipe for it in the next chapter.

Gather these supplies to make this recipe:

- **2 cups milk kefir.**
- **½ cup strawberries.**
- **½ cup vanilla ice cream.**
- **1 teaspoon vanilla extract.**
- **Fermenting vessel.**
- **Blender.**

Follow these directions:

1. Ferment a batch of kefir. You need fresh kefir for this recipe. Be sure to strain the kefir grains out before making this recipe.
2. Cut the strawberries into pieces.
3. Add the strawberries and the vanilla extract to the kefir in the fermenting vessel.
4. Place a lid on the vessel and let the kefir ferment for 12 to 24 hours.

5. Check the kefir periodically and transfer it to the fridge once it's fermented to your preference.
6. When you're ready to drink it, take the kefir and dump it in a blender. Add the ice cream and blend it into the kefir.

Orange Creamsicle Kefir

Ever since I was a kid, I've loved orange creamsicles. My father would take me to the corner store and would buy me one every Friday after school. I've had a weak spot for them ever since. I've since given them up, for the most part, because I'm trying to eat healthy. This recipe helps ease the pain when I find myself pining for a creamsicle.

If this recipe isn't creamy or sweet enough for you and you're able to tolerate unfermented dairy, try stirring some whipped cream into the kefir right before you serve it. It's sinfully delicious.

Again, if you decide to use honey, be sure to add it right before consuming the kefir. That way, it won't have time to kill any of the bacteria in the kefir.

Here are the supplies you'll need to gather to make this recipe:

- **4 cups milk kefir.**
- **1 tablespoon orange zest.**
- **2 teaspoons vanilla extract.**
- **Honey or stevia, to taste.**
- **Fermenting vessel.**
- **Blender.**

Here are the directions:

1. Use fresh kefir that's already been fermented 12 to 24 hours. Don't add the orange zest or vanilla until the kefir grains have been strained out.
2. Add the orange zest and vanilla to the kefir and stir it up.

3. Place a tight lid on the container and let it ferment for an additional 12 to 24 hours at room temperature.

4. Check the kefir and once it's fermented to your liking, move it to the fridge or consume it immediately.

5. When you decide to consume it, place the kefir in a blender. Add the honey, to taste, and blend it into the kefir. Add a handful of ice, if you want the kefir cold, and blend it in. This kefir can also be poured over ice.

Kefir Cultured Cream

Kefir grains can be used to ferment milk cream to make a tasty cultured cream that can be used to replace regular cream in recipes and to make butter. This cream tends to be a bit on the sour side. If you want cream that isn't as sour, shorten the ferment time to 12 hours.

The rest of the recipes in this chapter require use of this cream.

Here's the list of items you need to make kefir cream:

- **Milk kefir grains.**
- **A fermenting vessel.**
- **Heavy cream.**
- **A stainless steel fine mesh strainer.**

Follow these directions to make kefir cream:

1. Add the heavy cream and milk kefir grains to the fermenting vessel. You'll need 1 to 2 tablespoons of grains for every quart of cream you add.
2. Place a cloth cover over the container and secure it in place.
3. Let the cream ferment for up to 48 hours, checking it every 12 hours to see if it's ready. Stir the kefir each time you check it for best results.
4. Once the kefir cream has fermented to your liking, strain out the kefir grains and move them to fresh milk or cream.

5. Place a tight lid on the container or bottle it and move it to the fridge.

Kefir Cultured Butter

Kefir cream can be used to make tasty cultured butter. Once you try this butter, you might not ever want to eat regular butter again. Don't throw away the liquid that separates from the cream. That liquid is traditional buttermilk, the cultured version.

Here are the supplies you're going to need:

- **4 cups kefir cream.**
- **Stand mixer.**

Follow these directions to make kefir cultured butter:

1. If you're using freshly fermented kefir cream, place the kefir cream in a glass container in the fridge for 8 to 12 hours. This step isn't necessary if the kefir has already been refrigerated.
2. Take the cream out of the fridge and let it sit at room temperature for a couple hours.
3. Place the cream in the stand mixer bowl and attach the bowl to the mixer. Turn the mixer on a low setting in order to avoid splattering cream everywhere. Once the cream thickens, you can turn the mixer up, but watch the cream closely. Slow the mixer down again when butter starts to separate or you'll get buttermilk everywhere.
4. Let the mixer run on low until chunks of butter form. Pour off the buttermilk, pressing the butter to squeeze as much buttermilk out as possible.
5. Wash the butter with cold filtered water. Squeeze out as much buttermilk as possible during the washing process. If you leave too much

buttermilk in the milk, the butter will go rancid a lot faster than it will if you get most of the buttermilk out.

6. Once the kefir cultured butter is done, place it in a glass container with a tight lid and store it in the fridge.

Butter can still be made from kefir even if you don't have a stand mixer available. It's just going to take more work. If you have a good blender, you can blend the cream until it separates. The best blenders have multiple blades that extend up from the bottom and mix the cream throughout the entire canister. You can also churn the buttermilk by hand, but be prepared to work at it a bit.

Once you have kefir cultured butter, it can be used most places you'd use regular butter. Remember that cooking the butter will kill the probiotic cultures in the butter. That doesn't mean it isn't edible anymore; it just means it won't have the same health benefits as uncooked kefir butter.

Kefir Cultured Ice Cream

Here's a kefir cream recipe the kids in the family will love to make and eat. This recipe requires an ice cream maker.

Here are the supplies needed to make kefir cultured ice cream:

- **2 cups kefir.**
- **2 cups kefir cream.**
- **1 cup sugar.**
- **3 eggs.**
- **3 teaspoons vanilla extract.**

Here are the instructions you need to follow. The instructions may vary based on the type and brand of ice cream maker you're using. This recipe uses an electric ice cream maker:

1. Place the ice cream maker bowl in the freezer at least 12 hours in advance.
2. Whisk the kefir, the kefir cream and the vanilla together in a bowl.
3. In a separate bowl, whisk the eggs and the sugar together.
4. Combine the contents of the two bowls together and mix until smooth.
5. Place the ice cream maker bowl into the ice cream maker. Add the paddle to the inside of the bowl.
6. Turn the ice cream maker on and add the ice cream mixture to the ice cream maker bowl. Add

any additional ingredients you'd like to add at this time.

7. Put the lid on the ice cream maker and let it run until your ice cream is finished.

8. If you don't eat all of the ice cream, it can be stored in the freezer in airtight containers made to be frozen. It will last indefinitely because the fermenting process will completely stop.

This basic recipe can be used to make a ton of different types of ice cream. Here are some ideas to help you along:

- **Banana.** Before adding the ice cream mix to the ice cream maker bowl, place the mix in a blender with a couple ripe bananas and blend it until smooth.
- **Butterfinger.** Place a Butterfinger candy bar or two in the blender and blend it into small chunks. Add it to the ice cream maker when you add the ice cream mix.
- **Candy cane.** Add 1 teaspoon of mint extract to the ice cream mix and stir it in. Crush up a couple candy canes and add them to the ice cream maker at the same time you add the ice cream mix.
- **Cherry.** Halve and pit a handful of cherries and toss them in the blender with the ice cream mix.
- **Chocolate.** Add ¼ cup cocoa powder to make chocolate ice cream.
- **Peach.** Blend peaches into the ice cream mix or stir in peach preserves.

- **Peanut butter.** Add ½ cup chunky peanut butter to the mix and stir it in. Top the ice cream with peanuts.
- **Strawberry.** Add ½ cup of strawberry jam to the ice cream mix and stir it in to make strawberry ice cream.
- **Toasted almond.** Toast 1 cup of almonds by baking them on a cookie sheet for 10 minutes at 350 degrees F. Chop them up and add them to the ice cream maker at the same time you add the ice cream mix.

Kefir Cultured Cream Cheese

Here's yet another dairy staple that can be made with milk kefir instead of regular milk. This cultured cream cheese makes a delicious dip and can be used to replace cream cheese in a number of recipes. It doesn't taste exactly like cream cheese, but is close enough in taste and texture that it's a decent replacement at least some of the time.

The liquid left in the bowl is whey that can be used to inoculate all sorts of fermented foods. It can also be added to smoothies to give them a probiotic boost.

Here are the supplies you're going to need:

- **3 cups kefir cultured cream.**
- **Cloth.**
- **A large bowl.**
- **String.**

Follow these instructions to make kefir cultured cream cheese:

1. Find a square piece of cloth large enough to hold 3 cups of kefir. An old white t-shirt (washed, of course) can be cut up and used. Cheesecloth can also be used, but you're going to need at least 5 layers.
2. Place the cloth in the bowl, so the entire bowl is lined with the cloth.
3. Pour the kefir cultured cream into the center of the bowl, on top of the cloth. You can use regular milk kefir, but it needs to be fermented long enough to make it nice and thick.

4. Fold the corners of the cloth up to the center and tie them together using the string to create a bag containing the kefir.

5. Hang the bag in the fridge. If you can't hang it in the fridge, hang it in a cool area of your house. If you hang it somewhere warm, the kefir will continue fermenting at a rapid pace and may end up too sour.

6. Place the bowl beneath the bag to catch all the liquid that drips through the cloth.

7. Let it sit overnight.

8. The whey will separate from the kefir cream cheese. You'll be left with cream cheese inside the cloth bag and whey in the bowl. Place both the whey and the cream cheese in airtight containers and keep them refrigerated until you decided to eat them.

Kefir Ranch Dressing

There really isn't a whole lot you can do with milk or buttermilk that can't be done with kefir. Homemade ranch dressing tastes much better (and is better for you) than the ranch dressing you buy at the store. Yes, that includes the Hidden Valley Ranch packets. Once you try this ranch dressing, you might not ever want to go back to store-bought ranch again.

If this recipe is too thick, try adding a bit more kefir or even some milk to thin it out.

Here's the ingredient list:

- **1 cup real mayonnaise.**
- **½ cup kefir.**
- **½ cup kefir cultured cream.**
- **1 clove of garlic.**
- **4 tablespoons chopped parsley.**
- **2 tablespoons chives.**
- **½ teaspoon paprika.**
- **½ teaspoon oregano.**
- **Salt, to taste.**

Here are the instructions for homemade kefir ranch dressing:

1. Chop the garlic up as fine as you can chop it. Add the parsley, chives, paprika, oregano and salt to the garlic and mash it all together.
2. Combine the mayonnaise, kefir and kefir cultured cream in a bowl and stir it together.

3. Add the garlic paste to the bowl and stir it in until incorporated.
4. Chill for 3 to 4 hours before use.

Kefir Fruit Dip

I've served this recipe at parties with a large tray of fruit and it's been a huge hit. Strawberries, peaches, apples, cantaloupe and blueberries are all good choices to serve with this dip.

Here are the ingredients you're going to need:

- **1 cup kefir cultured cream cheese.**
- **½ cup milk kefir.**
- **3 to 5 tablespoons organic cane sugar.**
- **5 tablespoons pineapple juice.**
- **½ teaspoon cinnamon.**

Blend all of the ingredients in a blender. Place in a bowl and serve with a tray of fruit.

Kefir Guacamole

Kefir makes a great addition to guacamole. It adds a barely noticeable tang and gives it a slightly creamier texture than normal. It also adds probiotic bacteria to your guacamole. You can't ask for much more than that.

Here are the ingredients you're going to need to make kefir guacamole:

- **4 ripe avocadoes.**
- **2 cloves of garlic.**
- **3 tablespoons chopped green onions.**
- **1 medium tomato.**
- **2 tablespoons fresh lime juice.**
- **3 tablespoons kefir cultured cream.**
- **Cilantro, to taste.**
- **Salt and pepper, to taste.**

Follow these directions to make kefir guacamole:

1. Cut the avocadoes in half and remove the seeds. Scoop out the flesh and mash it up.
2. Mince the cloves of garlic.
3. Chop up the cilantro.
4. Dice the tomato.
5. Combine the mashed avocado with the rest of the ingredients and stir it all together.
6. Add salt and pepper, to taste.

Cultured Kefir Cream Frosting (Vanilla and Chocolate)

Here's a food most people wouldn't expect to be cultured: frosting. This recipe makes vanilla frosting. You could just as easily make chocolate frosting by adding a couple tablespoons of cocoa powder to the recipe. Be careful not to add the kefir while the chocolate is too hot or you run the risk of killing the good bacteria in the kefir.

Anything you frost with this frosting has to be stored in the fridge. Refrigerate it before serving it and keep any leftovers in the fridge.

Gather the following ingredients:

- **½ cup kefir cultured cream.**
- **3 cups powdered sugar.**
- **1 ½ teaspoons vanilla extract.**
- **¼ cup butter.**

Here are the directions:

1. Melt the butter.
2. Let it cool until it's lukewarm and stir the powdered sugar into the butter.
3. Add the cultured cream and the vanilla and stir quickly until the frosting thickens. A stand mixer can be used to make things easier.
4. Place the frosting in the fridge for 15 minutes to give it time to thicken.
5. If the frosting isn't thick enough after cooling in the fridge, add more powdered sugar and stir it in.

Non-Dairy Kefir

Some people can't handle dairy regardless of whether it's been fermented or not. For those folks, milk kefir made from fruit and nut milks may be the next best option. Non-dairy kefir gives you most of the benefits of kefir without the lactose and casein associated with dairy. Be aware that there may be traces of milk left on and in the grains that can be passed into this kefir, but the amount will be minimal. If you're highly allergic to dairy, water kefir grains are a better choice.

Kefir made from non-dairy milks tends to be on the thin side, so it doesn't always lend itself well to making recipes like kefir cultured butter, ice cream or cream cheese. What it does do is give you opportunity to pretty much eliminate dairy while enjoying the probiotic benefits of milk kefir. That alone is worth the price of admission for some folks.

Milk kefir grains prefer dairy milk as a food source, but can be used to ferment all kinds of non-dairy milk alternatives. It may take making a few batches of kefir before the grains grow accustomed to fermenting the new liquid, so be prepared to throw out a batch or two. Over time, you may find milk kefir grains grow weak when used to ferment multiple batches of non-dairy kefir. This doesn't always happen, but if it does the grains can usually be rejuvenated by moving them back to dairy for several ferments.

If used to make more than a handful of batches of alternative milk kefir, the grains will usually stop growing.

If you're looking to acclimate kefir grains to non-milk sources, it may be best to keep some grains on hand in cow's milk, so you'll have healthy growing grains if you need them.

Coconut Milk

This first recipe isn't for kefir. It's a recipe for coconut milk that can be used to make kefir. Contrary to what a lot of people believe, coconut milk isn't the juice found inside a coconut when you crack it open. Coconut milk has to be extracted from the meat of the coconut.

If you don't want to make your own coconut milk, you can buy it from the store, but I've found the best coconut milk kefir comes from homemade coconut milk.

Here are the supplies you'll need:

- **4 cups unsweetened shredded coconut.**
- **3 cups hot water.**
- **2 bowls.**
- **A strainer.**
- **Cheesecloth.**

Follow these instructions to make coconut milk:

1. Place the coconut in one of the bowls. Pour the hot water into the bowl with the coconut and stir the contents of the bowl.
2. Let the coconut sit until it cools to room temperature.
3. Place the contents of the bowl into a blender and blend it until the coconut is finely chopped.
4. Place the strainer over the other bowl and line it with 3 pieces of cheesecloth.
5. Pour the coconut into the strainer.
6. Lift the corners of the cheesecloth up to make a bag that contains the coconut. The liquid that

passes through the cheesecloth and drips into the bowl is coconut milk. Squeeze the cheesecloth to get as much of the coconut milk out as possible.

7. Store the coconut milk in the fridge until you're ready to use it. Keep the leftover coconut pulp and dry it out. It can be sprinkled on the coconut kefir when you serve it to add a bit more coconut flavor.

Coconut Milk Kefir

Now that you've got homemade coconut milk, you're ready to make coconut milk kefir. Since coconut milk kefir tends to be a bit thin, I add coconut cream to the recipe to thicken it up a bit. This ingredient is optional and can be eliminated if you don't mind thin kefir.

Here are the supplies needed to make coconut milk kefir:

- **2 cups coconut milk.**
- **½ cup coconut cream (optional).**
- **2 tablespoons milk kefir grains.**
- **A blender (optional).**
- **Fermenting vessel.**
- **A stainless steel fine mesh strainer.**

Here are the directions for making coconut milk kefir:

1. Combine the coconut milk and coconut cream. A blender works well. It can be done by hand, but you've got to be sure the cream and milk are completely combined. Skip this step if you don't want to use coconut cream.
2. Place the coconut milk and cream combination into the fermenting vessel. Fill the container ¾ of the way full.
3. Add the kefir grains and stir the contents of the vessel.
4. Cover the container with cheesecloth or cloth and secure it to the container by tying it or banding it.

5. Let the container sit at room temperature for 24 hours. Check it every 12 hours to see if it has fermented to your preference.

6. Once the kefir has fermented, strain out the kefir grains. Move the liquid to an airtight container or bottle and store it in the fridge.

Coconut Meat Kefir Spread

Make enough coconut milk and you'll be left with large amounts of coconut meat that's been drained of milk. The meat is tasty, but is packed with sugar and really isn't great for you to consume on its own. This meat can be combined with coconut kefir and fermented to reduce the amount of sugar in the coconut and make it a probiotic treat that can be spread on crackers or added to smoothies.

Here are the supplies you're going to need:

- **½ cup fresh coconut milk kefir.**
- **2 cups coconut meat.**
- **Fermenting vessel.**
- **A stainless steel fine mesh strainer.**

Follow these instructions to make coconut meat kefir spread:

1. Blend the coconut meat and coconut milk kefir together.
2. Place the blended meat and kefir in the fermenting vessel and place the lid on it.
3. Let the container ferment at room temperature for 24 hours.
4. Move the container to the fridge.

Thick & Creamy Coconut Milk Kefir

Coconut milk kefir is thin when made using traditional milk kefir fermenting technique. This recipe creates thick kefir that's the consistency of thick yogurt. You're going to have to eat this stuff with a spoon.

First, gather these supplies:

- **3 cups coconut milk kefir.**
- **Glass bowl.**
- **Stainless steel sieve.**
- **Cheesecloth.**

Here are the directions for making this recipe:

1. Place 8 to 10 layers of cheesecloth into the sieve. Alternatively, you can use cotton cloth or muslin cloth.
2. Pour the coconut milk kefir into the sieve and support the sieve so the liquid that drains from it drains into the bowl.
3. Place the bowl and the sieve in the fridge and let the coconut milk kefir drain through the sieve for 6 to 12 hours.
4. Check the kefir every few hours and move it to a glass container with an airtight lid when it reaches the consistency you want it to be.

Almond Milk Kefir

Milk kefir grains can be used to ferment almond milk. They typically can't be used more than a couple times to make almond milk kefir before they need to be rejuvenated in regular dairy milk. There are people who claim to have gotten milk kefir grains used to almond milk to the point where they can continuously use the grains solely in almond milk, but I've yet to see one in person.

I haven't been that lucky myself and am happy to get a couple batches of almond milk kefir before my grains start to get weak. Once I rejuvenate them for a batch of kefir or two in regular milk, they're able to be switched back to almond milk.

You're going to need the following supplies to make almond milk kefir:

- **4 cups almond milk.**
- **2 tablespoons milk kefir grains.**
- **Fermenting vessel.**
- **A stainless steel fine mesh strainer.**

Here are the directions:

1. Place the milk kefir and almond milk in the fermenting vessel and place a cloth cover on the vessel.
2. Let the kefir ferment for 24 to 48 hours.
3. Once the kefir has fermented to your liking, strain out the grains.
4. Place a tight lid on the container or bottle the kefir.

5. Move the container to the fridge until you're ready to drink the kefir.

Rice Milk Kefir

Rice milk is another alternative to dairy that can be used to make pretty good kefir. You can make rice milk at home by combining a cup of cooked rice with 3 to 4 cups of filtered water and a teaspoon of organic cane sugar and blending it for 5 minutes in a blender. For thicker rice milk that'll make thicker kefir, try adding more rice.

You'll need the following supplies to make rice milk kefir:

- **4 cups rice milk.**
- **2 to 3 tablespoons milk kefir grains.**
- **Fermenting vessel.**
- **A stainless steel fine mesh strainer.**

Follow these instructions to make rice milk kefir:

1. Add the rice milk and the milk kefir grains to the fermenting vessel.
2. Place a cloth lid on the container and secure it in place.
3. Let the rice milk ferment for 24 hours at room temperature.
4. Once the rice milk has fermented to your liking, strain out the kefir grains.
5. Place a lid on the container (or bottle the kefir) and store it in the fridge.

Fizzy Grape Kefir

Add milk kefir grains to grape juice and let them ferment and you get a fizzy grape kefir that has the benefits of grape juice and kefir combined into one tasty package. This is a good option for those in your family who don't like or can't handle dairy kefir.

You may find your kefir grains get weaker over time when using them to make grape juice kefir. Once you've switched kefir grains to grape juice, they don't generally do well when switched back to milk. Switch the grains and discard (or add them to smoothies) them when they lose effectiveness.

If you don't want to risk damaging your kefir grains, make fizzy kefir and add grape juice to it after you've strained out the grains.

Here are the supplies you'll need:

- **3 cups 100% Concord grape juice.**
- **2 tablespoons milk kefir grains.**
- **1 cup filtered water.**
- **Fermenting vessel.**
- **A stainless steel fine mesh strainer.**

Follow these directions to make fizzy grape kefir:

1. Rinse the kefir grains off.
2. Add the Concord grape juice, water and kefir grains to the fermenting container and stir them together.

3. Place a piece of cloth or cheesecloth over the container and secure it in place with string or a rubber band.

4. Let the kefir ferment at room temperature for 24 hours. Strain out the kefir grains once the grape juice starts to bubble.

5. Place a tight lid on the container and let it ferment for an additional 24 hours, or until the drink is carbonated to your liking. Open the lid to allow gases to escape every 12 hours.

6. Serve over ice.

Soy Milk Kefir

I really like soy milk kefir.

What I don't like is how hard it is to find organic non-GMO soy milk that doesn't have carrageenan in it, so I don't make it as much as I'd like to. Carrageenan is a food additive that's allowed in natural and organic foods because it's extracted from seaweed. It's used as a thickener and to add texture to food. For some people, that isn't all it adds. It's known to cause gastrointestinal distress and inflammation in some people. If you're having stomach problems (or other health problems, for that matter) and can't find the source, try eliminating carrageenan.

It may take a couple batches of soy milk kefir for your grains to get used to the soy milk. If you're using your grains for the first time to make soy milk kefir, it's recommended you toss out the first batch or two made with the grains to give them a chance to grow accustomed to the soy milk.

Here are the supplies needed to make soy milk kefir:

- **4 cups soy milk.**
- **2 tablespoons milk kefir grains.**
- **Fermenting vessel.**
- **A stainless steel fine mesh strainer.**

Here are the directions for soy milk kefir:

1. Place the soy milk and the kefir grains in the fermenting vessel and stir them up.
2. Place a cloth cover on the container and secure it in place.

3. Let the soy milk ferment at room temperature for 24 hours.
4. Once the milk has fermented to your liking, strain the kefir grains out of the soy milk.
5. Place a tight lid on the container or bottle the kefir and move it to the fridge.

Kefir Sauerkraut

There are a couple ways milk kefir can be used to make sauerkraut. The grains can be added to the fermenting container, as is the case with this recipe, or kefir whey can be used as a starter culture. Kefir whey is the clear liquid left over when you make kefir cultured cream cheese. Use ¼ cup of whey in the place of the grains.

It isn't recommended that you use the same grains you use to make milk kefir to make this recipe. If you have extra grains on hand and are looking for a way to use them, this recipe is a good choice.

Here are the supplies you need to gather:

- **2 tablespoons milk kefir grains.**
- **1 head of cabbage.**
- **1 tablespoon caraway seeds.**
- **Filtered water.**
- **Fermenting vessel.**

Here are the instructions for making kefir sauerkraut:

1. Wash the cabbage and chop it up. Lightly bruise the cabbage with a kraut hammer.
2. Place the kefir grains in the bottom of the fermenting vessel.
3. Add the cabbage on top of the kefir grains.
4. Add the caraway seeds.
5. Stir the sauerkraut up to mix the kefir grains into the sauerkraut.
6. Add filtered water until the cabbage is covered.

7. Place a weight in the container to keep the cabbage below the surface of the water. A folded up cabbage leaf can be pressed into the container. Glass weights are also available. Make sure to use a non-reactive material.

8. Place a tight lid on the jar and let the sauerkraut ferment at room temperature for 3 to 5 days. Make sure the cabbage stays beneath the surface of the water the entire time.

9. Once the sauerkraut has fermented to your liking, move it to the fridge and store it in an airtight container. Periodically open the container to allow gases to escape.

Milk Kefir as a Sourdough Starter

Sourdough starters need two groups of microorganisms: bacteria and yeasts. Milk kefir has a lot of both. The bacteria provide the sour flavor to the dough, while the yeasts create gases that help the bread rise. This recipe calls for kefir whey, which is the liquid you get when you strain kefir through cloth.

Here are the supplies you're going to need on hand to use milk kefir as a sourdough starter:

- **2 cups unbleached flour.**
- **2 cups milk kefir.**
- **Glass container.**

Here are the directions for making kefir sourdough starter:

1. Add the flour and kefir to a glass container and mix them together.
2. Place a tight lid on the container and let the container sit in a warm room for 2 to 3 days. You'll know the culture is ready when it starts bubbling.
3. Use this sourdough starter culture to make sourdough bread. It works with most sourdough recipes.

When you cook the bread, the probiotic bacteria in the kefir will die off. This recipe allows you to use kefir to make bread, but doesn't make bread containing probiotic cultures.

Storing Kefir Grains

There may come a time when you want to put your kefir grains away for a while and stop making milk kefir. The best method for storing your grains depends on how long you plan on storing them. Kefir grains can be stored for up to a year, depending on the method.

For short-term storage, your best bet is to place the kefir grains in a container of milk that you keep in the fridge. Use a cup of milk for every tablespoon of grains being stored for best results. The milk will last a week or two in the fridge. Swap the milk out once a week for best results. Leave the grains in the same milk for more than a week and they might start to starve.

Storing kefir grains long-term is possible. Grains can be stored frozen for a couple months. Rinse the grains off before freezing them and place them in an airtight container. Kefir grains can sometimes be stored for longer periods of time using this method, but may start to lose effectiveness after a couple months. The yeasts in frozen grains will eventually start to die.

Kefir grains that have been dried out can be stored for up to a year. Place the grain on a paper towel in a well-ventilated area of your house and let them dry until they're completely dried out. They will shrink and turn a yellow color when dry. Place them in an airtight container and move them to the fridge once they're dry.

When you decide to use frozen or dry grains, they have to be brought back to life. Move the grains to fresh milk and let them sit for 24 hours. Use ½ cup of milk for every tablespoon of grains. Replace the milk every 24 hours until the grains are active again. This can take 2 to 4 weeks if the grains have been stored for a long time.

Any grains that haven't revived within a month should be tossed out. They'll be a darker color than the rest of the grains and won't be elastic and growing. The longer kefir grains are stored, the more grains there will be that die and can't be brought back to life. Eventually the entire colony will die.

Kefir FAQ

This section is designed to answer many of the common questions people have about milk kefir. If you're having trouble with your kefir or have questions about the kefir-making process, chances are it's a problem or question other people have had as well. Check here before getting rid of your milk kefir or kefir grains.

Can Kefir Be Made In Non-Glass Containers?

The simple answer to this question is yes, kefir can be made in containers made of materials other than glass. You can make kefir in pretty much any type of container you'd like, but glass is your best bet because it's a non-reactive material that won't change the flavor or chemical composition of the kefir you're making.

Plastic can be used, but you run the risk of chemicals leaching from the plastic into your kefir. Ceramic is non-reactive, but there's a fairly high chance of lead being used in the glaze material. Metal shouldn't be used because the acids in kefir can react to the metal. Stainless steel is less likely to react, but there's still a slight chance of a reaction taking place.

Glass is your best bet. It's easy to clean, non-reactive and makes the best kefir. There isn't much of a cost difference between glass containers and the other materials, so glass is the way to go.

Can I Use (Insert Milk Name Here) to Make Kefir?

There aren't too many types of milk that can't be used to make kefir. Pretty much any animal milk sold in stores can be used, including cow, goat, sheep and buffalo milk. It can be made with most types of milk. The only type of milk I've had trouble with is ultra-pasteurized milk. Non-dairy milks like nut milks and soy milk can also be used.

If you aren't sure, the only sure way is to try to make kefir with the milk you're curious about and find out for yourself. If you're switching milk kefir grains from animal milk to an alternative milk type, it may take the grains a couple batches to get used to the new type of milk, so don't give up if it doesn't work right away.

How Fast Should Kefir Grains Grow?

It depends on the conditions the grains are kept under. Well-fed grains will add a quarter to their size during optimal conditions over the summer months. In cooler weather, this growth will slow to a crawl, even if the grains are being properly cared for and fed. 5% to 10% growth in the winter is the norm.

At times kefir grains will stop growing altogether. This is usually a stress response and is common with grains used to brew non-dairy kefir. As long as the grains continue producing good batches of kefir, the lack of growth isn't much of a problem as long as you take extra care not to lose any of your grains during the straining process.

Do Kefir Grains Need to be Washed Between Batches?

Kefir grains do not need to be washed before you move them from one batch of kefir to another. The only time the grains should be washed is if they're being moved from dairy milk to non-dairy milk that will be given to someone who is allergic to dairy. Be aware that there may be trace amounts of dairy on the grains even after you wash them.

If you do decide to rinse your kefir grains, do so with filtered water. The chlorine and fluoride in tap water can damage the grains and inhibit their ability to make kefir.

How Long Can Kefir Be Stored In the Fridge?

Kefir can be stored for a month or two in the fridge, but be aware it'll keep fermenting at a very slow pace. If you open the container and it smells off or doesn't taste right, it's best to discard the kefir and make a new batch.

Can Kefir Be Made Without Grains?

In a nutshell, no.

Fermented milk can be made without kefir grains, but it doesn't contain the same probiotic cultures and yeasts that true kefir has. The only way to make a product similar to kefir without grains is to use kefir starter packets, which are powdered kefir cultures. These cultures are usually only good for a handful of batches. No grains will be produced by kefir made using starter packets.

I Forgot to Move My Grains to New Milk. Can They Still Be Used?

Grains that are left in milk for too long can starve to death and will slowly start to die. Ideally, grains will be placed in a new container of milk every 24 to 48 hours. This will keep them constantly fed and will keep your grains happy.

If you forget to move your grains and they start to starve, they can sometimes be brought back to life. Take them out of the old milk and wash them off with filtered water. Place them in a new container of milk and let them sit for 24 hours. Replace the milk and let them sit for another 24 hours. Continue replacing the milk and letting the grains sit until they've rejuvenated.

I've heard of people rejuvenating grains that have been left in one glass of milk for three weeks. It wasn't easy, but they eventually came back to life and started producing kefir.

Can Kefir Be Used for Baking, Cooking, Etc?

Yes, with one caveat. Kefir can be used to replace milk in most recipes, but cooking kefir will kill off the probiotic cultures. You don't get anywhere near the health benefits from cooked kefir as you do uncooked kefir.

What Should I Do If There's Mold at the Top of the Container?

Mold and milk kefir aren't a good combination and are indicative of conditions that weren't conducive to the growth of good bacteria. If you find mold on your kefir or your kefir grains, discard the batch of kefir and the grains, even if the mold wasn't on the grains themselves.

Why Are My Kefir Grains Long and Stringy?

Kefir grains are living organisms that react to environmental changes. Grains can elongate and stretch out from time to time. This usually isn't indicative of a problem as long as the grains are still producing good kefir. Stringy grains are more common when the weather turns warm and room temperature increases.

Why Are My Kefir Grains Floating?

Floating kefir grains are usually a result of carbon dioxide trapped in the grain. The yeasts create carbon dioxide during the fermenting process, and when enough of it is trapped, the grains have been known to float to the top. This is normal kefir grain behavior and isn't a problem.

Damaged or dying kefir grains can also float. If your kefir is of poor quality and there are a lot of floating grains, this can be a sign of a dying colony.

What Is the Orange or Yellow Crust Forming on the Grains?

This crust can form for a number of reasons. Dried out grains will change color and start to form a crust. Fatty milk can also cause a crust to form. Try chopping crusted grains up or breaking them apart with your finger to expose areas of the grains that aren't covered in crust. A lot of the time, the crust can be washed away by placing the kefir in a bowl of water and rubbing it off.

How Much Alcohol Does Kefir Contain?

The amount of alcohol contained in milk kefir varies from batch to batch and is dependent on a number of factors. Kefir that's fermented for 12 to 24 hours will normally have less than 1% alcohol by volume. Longer fermentation times with tightly capped bottles will up the alcohol content.

Why Did the Taste and/or Texture of My Kefir Change?

Milk kefir grains are living organisms that are constantly changing and are largely a product of the environment in which they're kept. As such, the kefir your grains produce may vary in quality from batch to batch and will change over time and from season to season. This is one of the nuances of kefir and is something all producers of kefir have to deal with.

Keeping the temperature constant and keeping your kefir away from other fermenting foods can help avoid sudden unwanted changes. Kefir will vary in texture and taste based on how long it's fermented, the temperature at which fermentation takes place and the amount of grains used to ferment the milk. It's impossible to have complete control over your grains and the kefir they produce, so learning to accept change is imperative.

Why Did My Kefir Separate?

Separation is a normal part of the fermentation process. The longer kefir is allowed to ferment, the more likely it is to separate. Shorter fermentation times and fermenting at a cooler ambient temperature can help prevent separation. Fermenting with too many grains can also cause separation.

When kefir separates, it can be mixed back together and consumed. Strain out the grains and shake the kefir container up until the curds mix back into the whey. Kefir that has separated tends to be on the sour side, so you'll probably want to add sweetener before consuming it.

Contact the Author

I sincerely hope you enjoyed this book and are able to make use of the tips, techniques and recipes contained herein. I'd love to hear from you. If you have additional tips, techniques or recipes you'd like to see in future iterations of the book, send me an e-mail at the following address:

mike_rashelle@yahoo.com

I'll get back to you as soon as possible.

Other Books You May Be Interested In

In case you missed it, here's the first book in the fermenting series:

http://www.amazon.com/Fermenting-How-Ferment-Vegetables-ebook/dp/B00EKN7VS2/

Here's the second volume in the fermenting series:

http://www.amazon.com/Fermenting-vol-Fermented-
Beverages-ebook/dp/B00EPQWCPQ/

Essential oils are the concentrated essence of plants. Learn all about their many therapeutic qualities in the following book.

The Aromatherapy & Essential Oils Handbook

http://www.amazon.com/dp/B00BECCJXY

Diet plays a huge role in healthy living. If you're interested in healthy eating, there are a number of healthy foods you may be interested in adding to your diet. The following books may be of interest to you.

The Coconut Flour Cookbook: Delicious Gluten Free Coconut Flour Recipes

http://www.amazon.com/dp/B00CC0JFPM

The Almond Flour Cookbook: 30 Delicious and Gluten Free Recipes

The Quinoa Cookbook: Healthy and Delicious Quinoa Recipes (Superfood Cookbooks)

http://www.amazon.com/dp/B00B2T2420

The Coconut Oil Guide: How to Stay Healthy, Lose Weight and Feel Good through Use of Coconut Oil

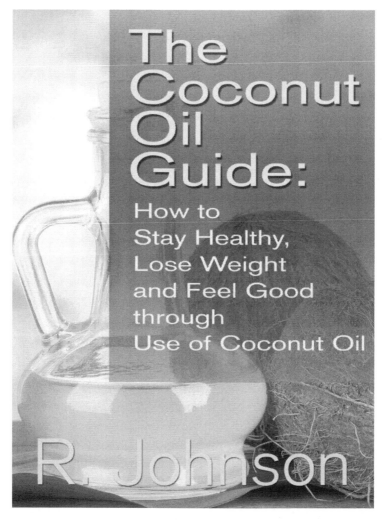

http://www.amazon.com/The-Coconut-Oil-Guide-ebook/dp/B00CESE3HC/